W9-ASO-535

FEB 1981
RECEIVED
OHIO DOMINICAN
COLLEGE LIBRARY
COLUMBUS, OHIO
43219

★ ★

WOMEN OF AMERICA

Harriet Tubman

BLACK LIBERATOR

MATTHEW G. GRANT

Illustrated by John Keely and Dick Brude

GALLERY OF GREAT AMERICANS SERIES

★ ★

Harriet Tubman

BLACK LIBERATOR

Text copyright © 1974 by Publication Associates. Illustrations copyright © 1974 by Creative Education. International copyrights reserved in all countries. No part of this book may be reproduced in any form without written permission from the publisher. Printed in the United States.

Library of Congress Number: 73-15849   ISBN: 0-87191-309-7

Published by Creative Education, Mankato, Minnesota 56001
Distributed by Childrens Press, 1224 West Van Buren Street, Chicago, Illinois 60607

LIBRARY OF CONGRESS CATALOGING IN PUBLICATION DATA
Grant, Matthew G
  Harriet Tubman.
   (Gallery of great American series. Women of America)
   SUMMARY: A biography of the famous conductor on the Underground Railroad who worked to free her people before, during, and after the Civil War.
   On spine: Harriet Tubman—Black liberator.
   1. Tubman, Harriet (Ross) 1815?-1913 — Juvenile literature. [1. Tubman, Harriet (Ross) 1815?-1913. 2. Negroes — Biography] I. Keely, John, illus. II. Title.
E444.T8974   301.44'93'0924 [B] [92]   73-15849
ISBN 0-87191-309-7

113335

CONTENTS

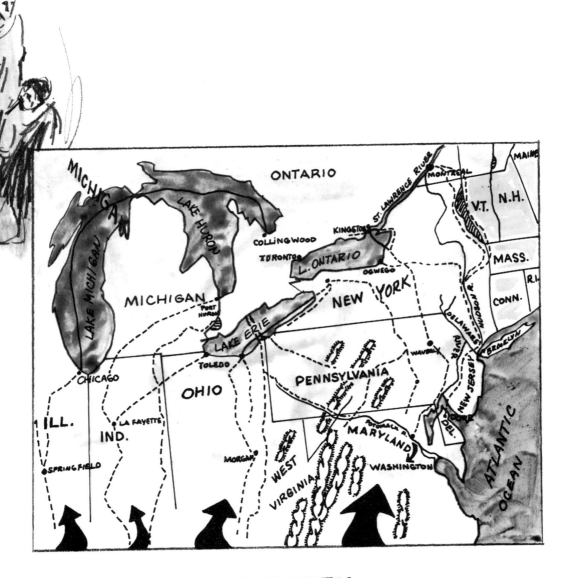

--- UNDERGROUND RAILROAD ROUTES

SLAVE GIRL IN MARYLAND

A slave girl, six years old, was considered old enough to work. So in 1826 little Araminta was taken from her mother and made to do housework. If she worked slowly, she was beaten.

Her mother, Old Harriet, and her father, Ben, could not do anything to help her. A slave that made trouble was apt to be sold. Life on a Maryland farm was hard—but there were much worse places.

Araminta's mother sometimes said: "You obey and stop being too uppity. Or else the Master's likely to sell you Down South where they'll work you to death."

But Araminta only scowled. She was a rebel.

At that time, slaves in the northern states were being set free. But not in the South. Cotton and rice crops needed slave labor. In

SLAVE GIRL IN MARYLAND

A slave girl, six years old, was considered old enough to work. So in 1826 little Araminta was taken from her mother and made to do housework. If she worked slowly, she was beaten.

Her mother, Old Harriet, and her father, Ben, could not do anything to help her. A slave that made trouble was apt to be sold. Life on a Maryland farm was hard—but there were much worse places.

Araminta's mother sometimes said: "You obey and stop being too uppity. Or else the Master's likely to sell you Down South where they'll work you to death."

But Araminta only scowled. She was a rebel.

At that time, slaves in the northern states were being set free. But not in the South. Cotton and rice crops needed slave labor. In northern states, preachers and writers called

Abolitionists called for an end to slavery.

Slave-holders replied: "Never!" And the stage

was set for a national tragedy that would erupt

in a terrible war some 30 years later.

Meanwhile, the slaves dreamed of freedom.

When she was about 13, Araminta saw a slave try to run away. She was in a country store at the time. A white man called out to her: "Stop that runaway!" But Araminta boldly refused to help.

The white man was so angry that he threw a heavy iron weight at her head. She was badly hurt and nearly died. For the rest of her life, she had "sleeping spells" that came and went in a strange way.

As a full-grown woman, Araminta was called Harriet, after her mother. She was only five feet tall but as powerful as a man. She chopped wood, cleared fields, and did a man's work for her master.

In 1844 she was married to a free black man named John Tubman. She dreamed of being free herself. But instead, she learned that she was going to be sold Down South, along with her three brothers.

UNDERGROUND RAILROAD

Her husband would not help her. But she had heard of the Underground Railroad to freedom. She thought it was a train that ran beneath the earth. She decided to find it and ride it northward.

Harriet Tubman's brothers started to run away with her. Later they became frightened

and returned home. But she went on, to the home of a kind white woman who had once promised to help her.

"The Underground Railroad is not really a train," the woman told Harriet. "It is a chain of houses. Each house is owned by people who hate slavery. The people there will shelter you, then pass you along northward."

Harriet traveled from house to house. Kind white people at the "railroad stations"

hid her and gave her food. Some drove her northward in wagons. At last she reached Pennsylvania, a free state. The sun was coming up. She stared at her hands to see if she was still the same person. Yes, she was still Harriet. But now she was free. Later she said: "I felt like I was in heaven. Free at last."

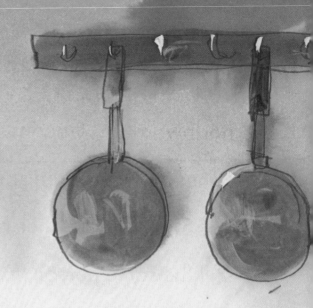

MOSES OF HER PEOPLE

Harriet could not forget her relatives left behind in slavery. She went to work in a hotel as a cook and saved money. She planned to go back to Maryland and rescue those she had left behind.

Harriet heard that her sister's family was to be sold. Brave Quakers snatched the hus-

band, wife, and two little children from the slave pens. Then Harriet met them in Baltimore and helped them travel the Underground Railroad to freedom.

In 1850, the Fugitive Slave Law was passed. Runaways were no longer safe in

northern states. They could be arrested. People helping them could be jailed.

But the Underground Railroad did not shut down. It simply extended its "stations" all the way to Canada. Harriet went back and rescued her brother and two other men. Then, in 1851, she went back to get her husband. But he had married again and refused to go North.

She was filled with grief and shame. But she could not "waste" her trip into danger-filled slave country. She gathered other slaves and took them to Canada.

She would perform such rescues many times in the years that followed. Harriet Tubman became the most famous "conductor" on the Underground Railroad. She would come up to a plantation and sing Let My People Go as a signal. Slaves crept away with her.

Dodging slave-hunters, suffering from hunger and exposure, she would lead her people from house to house for hundreds of miles—to safety in Canada.

The slaves called her "Moses" because she was like the prophet who took the children of Israel out of Egypt into the Promised Land.

The white slave-holders put a price on her head. Anyone who caught Harriet Tubman could claim a reward of $40,000. But nobody caught her. She said that God helped her to get out of tight spots. And Harriet herself was a master of tricks and disguises.

If a slave became faint-hearted and wanted to turn back, she would draw a pistol and say: "Go free or die." She knew that if a slave returned, he would be forced to betray the Railroad. But no slave ever insisted on going back. In 19 trips south, Harriet rescued some 300 men, women, and children.

She said: "I never run my train off the track. I never lost a passenger."

CIVIL WAR HEROINE

Harriet even managed to smuggle her [free]

aged parents to freedom. But many slaves in

the South still lived in misery. Many people

began to say slavery could only be abolished

through bloodshed.

The Civil War began in 1861. At first, President Lincoln was reluctant to come out against slavery. But the Union Army did not hesitate to enlist slaves and ex-slaves in the fight. Harriet Tubman herself joined the war in Port Royal, South Carolina. At first she was a nurse in a camp hospital. Later, she was asked to organize guerilla bands among the slaves in the area. She served as a spy and a scout for the Union forces.

On June 2, 1863, she guided a force of 300 black soldiers on a raid up the Combahee River. She was the real leader of the

attack, which destroyed Confederate supplies
and freed 800 slaves. Her exploit was written
up by eastern newspapers and she became
famous.

When the war ended in 1865, she was working at a hospital caring for freed slaves. Worn out, she went to Auburn, N.Y., where her old parents now lived.

The Thirteenth Amendment to the Constitution wiped out slavery in the United States. But Harriet saw that black people were still poor and uneducated. She opened her home to any poor black person who needed help. Later, she founded a rest home, selling vegetables to support the old and the sick who depended upon her.

Harriet Tubman died March 10, 1913. She was buried with full military honors.

GALLERY OF GREAT AMERICANS SERIES

INDIANS OF AMERICA
- GERONIMO
- CRAZY HORSE
- CHIEF JOSEPH
- PONTIAC
- SQUANTO
- OSCEOLA

EXPLORERS OF AMERICA
- COLUMBUS
- LEIF ERICSON
- DeSOTO
- LEWIS AND CLARK
- CHAMPLAIN
- CORONADO

FRONTIERSMEN OF AMERICA
- DANIEL BOONE
- BUFFALO BILL
- JIM BRIDGER
- FRANCIS MARION
- DAVY CROCKETT
- KIT CARSON

WAR HEROES OF AMERICA
- JOHN PAUL JONES
- PAUL REVERE
- ROBERT E. LEE
- ULYSSES S. GRANT
- SAM HOUSTON
- LAFAYETTE

WOMEN OF AMERICA
- CLARA BARTON
- JANE ADDAMS
- ELIZABETH BLACKWELL
- HARRIET TUBMAN
- SUSAN B. ANTHONY
- DOLLEY MADISON